I0813225

Seabeast

Also by Rajiv Mohabir

Poetry

The Taxidermist's Cut

The Cowherd's Son

Cutlish

Whale Aria

Nonfiction

Antiman: A Hybrid Memoir

Translation

I Even Regret Night: Holi Songs of Demerara

Seabeast

Rajiv Mohabir

Four Way Books
Tribeca

Library of Congress Cataloging-in-Publication Data

Names: Mohabir, Rajiv, author.
Title: Seabeast / Rajiv Mohabir.
Description: Tribeca : Four Way Books, 2025.
Identifiers: LCCN 2025003856 (print) | LCCN 2025003857 (ebook) | ISBN 9781961897489 (trade paperback) | ISBN 9781961897496 (ebook)
Subjects: LCGFT: Poetry.
Classification: LCC PS3613.O376 S43 2025 (print) | LCC PS3613.O376 (ebook) | DDC 811/.6--dc23/eng/20250207
LC record available at https://lccn.loc.gov/2025003856
LC ebook record available at https://lccn.loc.gov/2025003857

This book is manufactured in the United States of America and printed on acid-free paper.

Four Way Books is a not-for-profit literary press. We are grateful for the assistance we receive from individual donors, public arts agencies, and private foundations including the New York State Council on the Arts, a state agency.

We are a proud member of the Community of Literary Magazines and Presses.

Contents

for Corinne Elizabeth Hyde

चन्द्र उदये समाधूतम् प्रतिचन्द्र समाकुलम् ।
चण्ड अनिल महाग्राहैः कीर्णम् तिमि तिमिम्गिलैः ।।

At moonrise, the ocean
reflecting countless orbs, leapt.

The water filled with wind-
swift crocodiles and whales.

—*Ramayana,* Yuddhakanda 4.114

Nu ic fitte gen   ymb fisca cynn
wille woðcræfte   wordum cyþan
þurh modgemynd   bi þam miclan hwale.

Now a song   of a kind of fish
I tell in words,   crafted into verse,
From memory   of that great whale.

—"The Whale"

Auctor systematis a particularibus ad universalia
adscendat; Doctor vero contra a generalibus
ad specialia descendat.

The author of *The System of Nature* ascends
from the detail to the universal. The scholar
descends from the general into the specific
(genus, species).

—Carolus Linnaeus

Ambulocetus natans

—Kuldana Formation fragments in matrix—

"walking whale"

"swimming"

fat pads

for hearing

brackish water powerful tail

jaw

femur

tibia

tooth

hind limbs

thrashed prey the remains

nearly complete

but no matter, I still

gouge my feet when I keep up

the silence of night,

halleluhu hallelujah as a crown.

We were misnamed

terror in American streets. My
mother calls

at least my brother,

we burn to remake
what foreignness obscured

stalking what prayers we can—

Atlantic White-Sided Dolphin

Lagenorhynchus acutus

I walked the curled fishhook
of the Cape into a cove
and found washed up

on a February shore,
the carcass, its grey whitened
with bird shit, eyes

missing, a new blowhole pecked
into its skull. Did it ignore

kin and pod though they
cried out in fall sun,

Come home, Come home
seeking instead a short-lived joy?

I have taken this other
world for my own—

morphed into a haramkhor,
eater of evil: who rips out
pages of the creation story. Once

the sea was a sea
of milk. Once summer
was a sea

of men. I remember
there was water
until I drank,

reckless, my beard soaked
and dropping diamonds.
After the beginning, a pause,

the silence
of winter ice,

the silence of night
meeting night.

Basilosaurus cetoides

The bones of this "lizard king"
with external ears and tympanic
bulla were so plentiful
did my great greats too
use them as furniture
in the nineteenth century
while Britain continued
to *discover* the rest of the globe?
We were misnamed
again and again: first *Hindu*,
then *Hindoo*, then *Indian*, then
Coolie, all subhuman
much like this precursory cetacean
of the Eocene, named
in Latin *great lizard*—
anguilliform, what to make
of twist and tear, teeth
gnashing sharks and durodons
into pulp, judged by fossilized
gouges in enamel and finger
holes on skulls. J—'s ancestors
from northern Germany
played bone flutes
for their dead at gravesites

their descendants
one day exhumed
in perfect pentatonic scales.
In Boston, before he left me,
his DNA results: a five-note
score against the bedframe,
now just a recalled strain
in the dark. What of my own
ancestors can be revived—
another *wastebasket taxon*,
us unnamed hoard of no future
everyone stops keeping notes.

Blue Whale

Balaenoptera musculus

Earth's biggest animal shares
its name with the mouse,

which means their every note
gives muscular song, wails, a small notion

here weighing one hundred
and seventy tons, which means

this moves you. This clay dome
bears a sea of light where

a simple pinprick and a nova burst,
swallowing any shadow or chimera.

It's pneumatically driven
membrane vibrations oscillate

air from larynx to cranial sinuses
to orchestrate a score. But why a joyful noise

without phonic lips, the staff
and ledger lines blank, free of treble?

You are built for music: a viola strung
with fiber and filament. It's how blue whales

voice the loudest song, not from deep
muscle, but from sliding breath:

a second nature that echoes blues, grace-
noting from extinction to a choral body.

Boto

Inia geoffrensis humboldtiana

Pink from skin abrasions
the boto lives in the Orinoco
River. Largest of the river
dolphins, sexually dimorphic
more than any other cetacean
species, its cervical vertebrae
are not fused which allows
the head a ninety-degree pivot.
Its skull is asymmetrical;
its beak is long with heterodont
teeth, conical for grabbing
piranhas, turtles, and crabs
and also teeth for crushing prey.
Unlike the *Platanista,* the boto
river dolphin's eyesight
is remarkable both underwater
and above the surface yet
it relies on biosonar for understanding
its relation to the riverbed,
fallen trees, prey schools,
and other botos. In human form,
skin still pink, I hide
my blowhole under my beanie
and go to charm another human

mate. I've stopped singing
in public restrooms after doctors
reset my broken and rebroken nose,
after echoing *swim this stream*,
my asymmetrical face still
grabbing at men on the E train.

Bowhead Whale

Balaena mysticetus

"Bowheads can sing two or three quite different songs at the same time."
—Hal Whitehead and Luke Rendell in *The Cultural Lives of Whales and Dolphins.*

I hold you, an un-dorsaled fetish,
against winter, thick black,
dreaming of sea's crushing quiet.

My head is the bow
    of a viola or voilà, my bones
ballad sailor-tales and my fluke
    smashes every vessel

Every morning you pour taxonomic
difficulty into your cup, two hundred
fifty-year-old spear points in your back.

that dares dissonance.
    Or do you bow down before
a trying tide or a trying
    whale on your ship's bow,

You ask of the scene on the mug,
can a whale be confused for "right"
if as the seamen lance him

or knot flesh ribbons,
a macabre bow, or to string
it with arrow or lance
so that whether by fluke—

thinking he'd float, their ship's bow
splits into flotsam; the baleen giant
turning from commodity into danger?

anchor or cetacean—
or fair weather you can tie
my tail to the hull
and cleave my fat from muscle

I say, *Even love breaks apart*,
and smash the ceramic, its slivers, ice
floe, sharp and disappearing. Now

and cleave to coin
        upon shoring up to market?
My any minute fin-
        flip a grave, split-

copepods vanish quickly,
the Arctic water clears—
What will sustain your gravity?

second error that leads
        to coffin. A wave rocks,
unsteadying your boat to smash it
        against ice-rock. Ship-

After silence comes silence.
I starve after your barrels of oil
and tongue my lips

board now foam, why did you
        ever board this vessel
of blood, picking my gore,
        goring me with explosive iron?

but they're bitter. You splinter
my schooner; from the crow's nest
I grip a harpoon.

Bryde's Whale

Balaenoptera brydei and *Balaenoptera edeni*

A catch-all species,
scientists believe others
belong to, like the misnamed
Omura's Whale or the Gulf
Bryde's Whale. Pronounced
broo-deh, not *bride.* The two
known species differ
only marginally in skull
shape and veil color, but
there is so much
we do not know
like who will be renamed
when more information emerges
from the depths
into anchovy shoals or
when two men marry and diverge?
What will it look like to redownload
Grindr or Scruff a decade
after I first put myself
inside you? What will I call you
tomorrow? The next day? In five years?
You were once beautiful
as my bride. The name for us
changing and changeable,

a wedding ring a bottom-
less basket.

California Sea Lion

Zalophus californianus

Your howlings begin plaintive
then roar. You muscle,
joy and sinew to wend
from rock into blue delight—
Shaitan, you twist to unhook fish
from men's lines cast. The casters
hate your ears but dress wives
in your fur. They profit
from your wind of foreflipper
and swish. *I'm three-quarters tired*
of performing for crowds
you say and dive. Imagine
before plumping to seven
hundred seventy pounds,
you feared the element
that allows agile grace. I want
buoyancy like you, immunity,
but as a man-of-war, a squid:
mythic and pursued. Once
your hands were opened
to my hands. I gave you
a carved stone—
red and gold like rays bleaching
your beard. I wanted

your teeth to puncture
my bone. Be valiant, pup,
glide and gambol
amid aquatic crash,
bark and clapmatch. Good, free
boy. The sea will change you
not into barrels of oil
but into floundering bliss.
No one will inflate
your streamlines into catamaran,
sealing season is done
so free your flip
among kelp beds—
Flop on the sand, the sea
crystals on your fur,
on your hair of flax,
king of mischief,
cheating lover.

Common Bottlenose Dolphin

Tursiops truncatus

Speaking of the anthropomorphic,
the bottlenose captures

and forces sex with others, acts out
impulses with the dead,

the inanimate, or with others,
for what I imagine to be

fun: penis in blowhole—
I know I would try it if I

had a blowhole. Well, actually
if I had *that kind* of blowhole.

But what do I know
of *Tursiops* communication or intelligence;

but what words we can ascribe
to their toys of eel grass

and plastic waste? They use tools,
adopt other species of dolphin,

have names, and like to get high,
did you know? New discoveries

shock me, like dolphins
tasting their friends' urine

to get to know them, though
I also understand this gay impulse.

Costero

Sotalia guianensis

Also called a Guiana dolphin
because of its coast hugging
and riverine disposition,
the Costero's shape echoes
a bottlenose except
it's just under seven feet
long and so terrified
of humans it flees from boats
at the slightest whir
despite being a true
Delphinidae: estuarine and
electroreceptive from Nicaragua
to Brazil. Its cousin the Tucuxi
may be more of a sister
or faggoty sibling: pink skin
to the Costero's blue. In fact
scientists only recently
rent these two sub-species
into distinct kinds—
but who knows if they breed
or produce viable offspring?
There is no "true" of any order.
It's easy for one brother to say
to Abel, *I am not your brother*;

how easy to be mistaken
for something you are
that not even scientists can
differentiate from another.

Devilfish

Eschrichtius robustus

In Baja a grey whale,
drawn by kisses and pets,
kidnaps tourists,

hoists their boat
on its back into a joy
ride, not yet understood

for its danger,
for the rarity of two hours
or the cobalt wake

blooming into morning
glory after
glory,

the proximity a wonder
for one, herald of demise
for the other.

How quickly whale
watching replaced hooks
and tryworks,

this devilfish turns
its eye to meet yours,
and sees a better world,

sees the miracle
of your skin
as if to offer absolution,

after our gifts of exploding
tips, of plastics, of acoustic
smog, it still reaches up—

And you cannot
yet forgive at least
your brother.

Dorudon serratus

When the Sahara was a sea,
every whale killed. Even in
the Tethys Sea. Basilosaurus' prey
was dorudon, its own relative.
When the poles froze the fish
stocks and the sea changed
and futurity laughed, bearing
its mammalian fangs like
scimitars in an ice-yawn. Today
cousins still kill one another
and durable ice grows between
brothers like between me and mine
when his Orlando number
doesn't shake my cell after
the latest mass murder where straight
men shot queers in Central
Florida. You would think
someone would give in and call
but his church cut our line—
Look at Cain. Look at Abel. Are
my prayers more pleasing
than yours, brother? Is that why
you threatened to kill me, in Jesus's
name? Which siblings are meant

for peace if the God of Biology,
God-as-Coolie-father,
designs us to compete?

False Killer Whale

Pseudorca crassidens

"Death is far from instant: first dolphins endure paralysis, then they die of gradual shock, hemorrhage, drowning, or asphyxiation."
—Susan Casey *Voices in the Ocean: A Journey into the Wild and Haunting World of Dolphins*

We pray with our lips. The ocean
is *terra nullius* its inhabitants
in black fish skins. An oceanic dolphin,
like its namesake kills and eats
other cetaceans and yet is known
to offer divers the fish they catch.
American corporations like Sea World
pay fisherfolk for mercury-
poisoned meat and for scouting
the calves. At the amusement parks
signs read *dolphins live longer*
in captivity, are *at danger in the wild.*
I call this a pseudo-concern
for conservation, funding slaughter
for the laughter of tail-splashed
tourist crowds. These back-flipping
black beasts were separated
as infants from families

of up to forty, sent away to board
in shallow tanks, after whalers
drove spikes into their mothers' blowholes,
severing spines and calf from mother
yet the *Pseudorca* nuzzles
the swollen bellies of pregnant women
who pay extra to ride their backs.

Fastitocalon

Once upon a lookout   gulls careened from the country
of myth to our world of flood.   I have been fooled by feather
        and scale alike. Sea-dizzy   with land-want when upon
the back of a man I stepped,   he refused my weight
        despite the silence I invited   into the blown-out lantern

of my mouth. The story   morphed its flippers and now
my rime of hoarfrost crusts   darkrooms. Like how *weorold*
        in Saxon means *world,*   *waeter* means *water*—together,
ocean. The Saxons   misheard the Greek *aspidochelone,*
the word itself a metaphor   transformed into *the great whale*

with land upon its back.   How each ship turned
into corpse-box, how   my pine will burn
        until I am but pearl.   O how blessed are the meek?
I've been hesitant to step   on loam since. Is this siren-lock
        or meremenn-haer; sea-   weed or fleót-wyrt? On my grave

will meós or moss grow;   the fable of evolution and
descent, from   weoroldwaeter to land,
        baleful the man-   ness, a toxicity we descend into,
brōþru / bhrātā   / brother?

Fin Whale

Balaenoptera physalus

Melville's razorback,
second to the largest
whale in the world, at
eighty to one hundred
sixty thousand pounds, means
there's some blue bigger
than you. You crave
recognition, I know why
you migrate far from home,
I am a second child—
never the record
even though at forty-four
and seven inches
taller than my brother,
whose own ex-family
is four more people
than mine which includes
me, my dog, and cat. I tried
to but couldn't impregnate
my ex-husband because
Science muttered something
about biology, which once said
man is *man* but now says
distinctions are more arbitrary;

a Western Rational episteme
which also held brown folks
as less-than-sub-human,
and in this razor-
country, my brown Caribbean
parents, both born before
1965, are still excluded
from America's settler dream.

Franciscana

Pontoporia blainvillei

Named for the grey
clad friars who prayed
for the well being
of animals as Christians ravaged
the Charrúa people with bible
pages and syphilis,
this five-foot estuary
cetacean swims southeastern
rivers and brackish waters
of South America. In Argentina
a crowd pulls a calf
from the surf each clicks selfie
after selfie to tweet, passing
the thing from hand
to hand until
its greasy skin dries and
it perishes, gasping
from dehydration,
smiling all the way
into demise—

Heavenly father,
They have trust in us
as we have in You; though
they owe us nothing.
Grant our prayer
through intercession of good
St. Francis of Assisi,
teach us to be deserving.

Ganges River Dolphin

Platanista gangetica gangetica

Herald of deluge, it side-
swims before the makara
to announce the goddess
Ganga's descent to earth.
But some confuse its long
pointed rostrum for
the makara, her vehicle:
this misnomer a limitation
of mythic imagination. Blind,
this *Platanista* paints murals
with echoes—the sacred river
was once glacial ice, the ice
was once sea, was once cloud—
it swims through the Bhojpuri
belt from Kanpur through Bihar,
and understands location
with an ultrasonic ping
of clicks. With all this talk
I remember my Aji, named
Gangadai not a dolphin
but a river that wound
far from the riverhead,
the place where she began,
a river I announce, though

my brown body's illiterate
of the old ways of rice planting
and floodplains, though
in my studio apartment—
location Paikō Lagoon,
Oʻahu—I know which songs,
endangered by entanglement
in fishing nets, hunting
for its aphrodisiac oil,
poisoning, and broken
prayers to sing in paddy fields,
though I sing them
with my American accent,
an echo of what was
before it melted, filled
with silt, broken clay pots,
dead bodies, runoff,
and raced
to the delta and sea

and then to cloud.

Grey Whale

Eschrichtius robustus

I.

Refugio Beach: close
to the bay's break,
                    a spout

as we sift rock and egret
carcasses for ossified refuge,
the stone
    bone becomes.

Great Pliocene cetacean frets
now unrecognizable,

petrified gestures: spy-
hop and side-
                              graze
in the backdrop.

II.

I sewed a fetish to your shirt,
a figurine to carry
        that ensures return.

You leave this season
to plough the sand bed,
                    mouth open,

to tongue amphipods,
          worms, sand fleas.

What remains
after you travel alone
                    up the coast?

III.
But for now our every breath:
a sudden burst. Your slack-

keyed baleen slat frays.
I am careless music too,

fingers curl around your fossil;
strum your spume, clumsy;

your palm prints: treble

clefts against shale cliffs,
our bones trading calcium
                    for agate's coda.

Gulf Whale (Rice's Whale)

Balaenoptera ricei

Once named for the whaler
who peeled your flesh
into bible-sized books,
you're a sea orange whose rind
spirals and unravels into a strip
of gore. Now with a distinct
three-ridged skull, you fill
your lungs before folding
pleura and bronchi into a deep,
plunging sound. Do you mean
to draw in pills of beaded crude
and misshapen crabs with no eyes
or apocalyptic claws: an orchestra
of woodwinds and brass bells
brimming with blood? You croon
dirges of the dead. The Gulf
is a web of submarine calls:
metal bodies and seismic air gun
surveys that scour the seafloor
for oil, a series of blasts that damn
your throat to the abyss though
Corexit lesions on your skin gape,
mouthing a black *Holy Holy Holy*
as your own oil spills from your ears

and ass. The hymn's notes break
off the staff as whole note
skimmers and soon fade into sky.

Hawaiian Monk Seal

Neomonachus schauinslandi

To reintroduce species
of the class *Phocidae*
to the bigger islands
of the Hawaiian archipelago
from the kūpuna islands,
from Laysan, Midway, Kure Atolls,
proves a threat to fishermen
on Oʻahu as the seals would rather
run the line than pray for recovery
even if their heads resemble monks
with their short hair. Sealing
diminished them once and yet
another kind of sealing emerges
from the Pacific. In Waikīkī
at Kaimana Beach, I see three
grow algae on their fur
basking in ultraviolet before
their awkward shamble back
into blue. Foraging plasticity
allows their diet, peppered
with squid, octopus, and crustaceans
to be complimented by plastic
reaching its tendrils from the Great
Garbage Patch to choke

ʻĪlio-holo-i-ka-uaua, little-dog-
that-runs-on-the-waves,
so I get why they attack tourists
who don't care about brown
suffering and want their canned
pineapple and still flock to Hawaiʻi
when Kānaka say a clear ʻaʻole.

Hawaiian Spinner Dolphin

Stenella longirostris

In ʻŌlelo Hawaiʻi: *naiʻa*
sounds like *naia* which
in Hindi means *new* which
in English means *renewal*
and *baptism*. Amma,
who mucked up your water
with this Sita-Savitri crap:
Good Indian women don't leave
their husbands no matter what?
Remember the catamaran
north of Puʻuhonua o Hōnaunau
when you left Pap's betrayals
again and again, someone
else's perfume staining your pillow?
You were afraid first but jumped
in after you saw dolphins flip
and twist in the sun, sky-clad
shaking off topaz.
You dove into the web
of their woven voices:
chirps and clicks that you felt
inside your throat. In the motion
of one hundred fifty bodies,
peace was with you; Amma,

named, *Shanti, Shanti, Shanti,*
lend me your grace, your new spin
as I leave my own husband.

Humpback Whale

Megaptera novaeangliae

Holy men gossip folktales
into religious texts.

We are immersed in the most
ancient of songs

ear to hull, the sea tongue
lashes rope and wind.

How with a push of rostrum
the whale guides others

to safety. Now humpbacks
are *altruists* born of humanist theory.

To know the whale,
we must first name it;

speak our will into its flesh,
enumerate all the ways to kill.

O great god, may you be saved
from human language.

Hybrid Unidentified Whale

Is it any shock that in loneliness
we compensate? How emptiness
is like a coral, a something,
that strews its intestines
then chokes another head
with its greedy bowels.
Poets gather at this bed, drawn
like rorquals to krill blooms,
to the metaphor's perfume
of being the first or the only
of one's own kind. Scientists listen:
a blue or fin? Or is it a sei? A mix
of the dying out? Whatever
beast calls out will never
know itself through the mirror
of another, as populations collapse
and the sea empties and no others
can process its cries into music.
I want to cast such song-frequency
with lines about how shells
gouge my feet when I keep up
with you foot for foot,
or how I've noticed
that you stop looking back

for me, or how I wish there were
a *you* behind the blue, but researchers
can no longer hear it strain or
its strain. Sometimes I call
into the abyss for so long
it reaches back and slides
down my throat.

Iberian Orca

Orcinus orca

Following the bluefin migration,
with their own languages, dialects,
and cultures passed from elders
to youth in a cycle of learning
that humans cannot understand
outside of terms such as *mimicry*
and *subhuman*, this subspecies
swimming the Northern Atlantic
in matriarchal groups revolt against
patriarchal lines dangling
in the water, extending to the new
form of hunting, scientists are split
as to the reason that draws the killers
to damage the vessels' rudders
and to sink fishing boats: *play* or
revenge—a behavior whale
watchers fear will spread across
the damaged world despite orca
type, residents, mammal-eating
transients, and those deep-dwellers,
when off the Shetland Islands
an orca rams a yacht. Or at least
we understand it as a need for justice.
Humans plot revenge ourselves,

our impulse to see the world as we are.
When a hornet stung my head,
out of want, I bought a smoker
to stun its kin underground until
I could flood them out with soap
and water, drowning them until
the earth no longer hummed underfoot.
Don't ask me where I learned this
thirst. My first sub blowjob? Video
games? Marriage?

Indian Humpback Dolphin

Sousa plumbea

The astrologer placed
on my pinky an emerald
to wear to ward off
Mercury's malefic effects,
recessed in my birth chart.
Inside this Jaipur cut jewel
a dark fleck I thought
trapped evil. I was
a coconut afloat in the sea
leaving *God's own country*.
I wanted to drown
my sinful self in the jade curls
of salt-waves; the shadow
wasn't evil at all
but wonder. From Kanyakumari
I took the rail up Kerala
and into Varkala where
from a clay cliff I watched
a pod of black *Sousa plumbea*
spout then leap obsidian
and falcate dorsals
in the rice paddy sea
freeing selves to green.

Indohyus indirae

Men laugh thick coat
in mats and fat store

but no matter, I still
pull dicks, my bones

thick, help me submerge
to escape. Their words

are little danger-
fires at midnight

when I can't wind
into sleep. This "Indian pig,"

this raccoon-sized ancestor's
foreskin layer soon

blubbers and may
or may not be a transitional

fossil scientists crave
even though it's simple to grasp

the need for aquatic life.
A predator from the street

or the sky casts its shadow
on my frame what choice

have I but to plunge
until ectotympanic bone

morphs into a diver's ear—

Irrawaddy Dolphin

Orcaella brevirostris

Beluga-shaped
but grey of skin

not true riverine
but brackish,

of this oceanic
shushuko is said

to understand
human speech

as though it's
urgent they

understand
our human universe.

From the Sundarbans to
the Mekong

to the Irrawaddy,
these toothed whales

were known for
    herding shoals of fish

    for fisherfolk
in whose nets

they now drown.
    The World Wildlife

    Federation reports
only ninety-two

individuals
    remain.

    Learning human
language opens you

to betrayal. Trust me
    though I am no

    hairless dolphin—
I once had a husband.

Ketea Indikoi

Come night
we count the animals
stitched together,
emerging from Paikō
Lagoon to graze—
hybrids of ram, lion,
and me Aryan,
Dravidian, Coolie, and
other things I can't chart
nautically in the wild
limu flares of the dredged
wetland. A puffer fish bloats
with macabre gas.
I'm puzzled by belonging
and not, by being a shadow,
a story about sea
travel, a sleight of eye or
the light, stitched
of many parts. Here, I am
wolf; here, snake. But this
is not South India and before
this my hair was curly,
my eyes fish-round.
I want to wind

my coils around trees
to shake dates
down to feed you,
my sweet, before
I plunge into a dawn
sea, glowing pink
and orange, a beautiful
danger. Quick
lick my palm before
any man sees and tries
to iron me out, to make
my body a single body,
legible by picking the spines
out of my head
one by one until
I am nothing
of myself.

Makara

Victory to the crab or
to the half-stag half-elephant,
fish, seal, lion-
footed Capricorn vahana
of riverine Ganga-Mata,
victory to you, Vedic hybrid
air breather, berth of Varuna
god of the sea, guardian of doorways
and thresholds, sigil of Kamadeva,
god of love, mother of Makaradhwaja
victory to the oceanic dragon,
etymological ancestor to the gharial,
magarmach, though
you are mammal of both
saltwater and river, crocodilian
jaws, chaos churn of delta-
mouth, victory to you
possible Gangetic Dolphin
or *Ambulocetus*, walking whale
who beholds even the Lord
Buddha, the earring
of Vishnu, preserver
of us all, Victory,
Sri Makar ki
jai.

Manatee

Trichechus manatus latirostris

"O Great Ancestors! Teach us
how to love our enemies."
—Jeffrey Yang

I.

Known by their scars, *manus*,
Latin for hand, *manti*, Taíno for breast,
these paddle-tailed sirenians
range from West Africa to the Caribbean
and once in 1995 one was spotted
in Cape Cod, this time not as a Columbian
mermaid—the Dugong is the siren
with the fluked tail. *Latirostris's*
prehensile snout grasps for hyacinth
and other plants in Floridian
spring fed rivers, clear as topaz,
where their numbers decrease yearly—
predated on by human vessels and Red
Tide. As a child I remember
a naturalist's whisper, *every living sea cow*
bears a disfigurement scratched by human propellers.
Floridians know this and still refuse
to install skegs onto their boats.

II.

Once on the Gulf Coast, like any common
sailor, I mistook a breath and dark

head for a person in six foot deep
water, a mother and calf with backs

written on with the cruelest ballad—
they approached the canoe. I wish

for such gentleness too, that I too
learn how to forgive enough to approach

my brother. But what is ever gentle
in a family? My first memory: Pap grabs

his riding crop and the resulting
black welts, *You're not going to be able*

to sit for a week, his curse to E— and me,
who learned to spy on each other,

competing for whatever cabbage-
shred of affection. Still,

some men's marks identify—
hide in the heart's deepest riverbeds:

E— writhing under Pap's cane,
his *manti* empurpled by Pap's *manus*,

for lying about a sixth-grade
science project deadline. Good marks

meant no skin marks. Did I smile when
Pap got the school's call and I knew

that I would be the day's golden son?
I don't remember. Regret clouds as Red Tide,

and still I hear his eleven-year-old
pleading *Sorry. Please I'll be good—*

and Amma just watches, saying nothing.

Minke Whale

Balaenoptera acutorostrata

The most abundant rorqual
arrow shaped, scientists now find

to rumble, growl, groan, grunt.
You can listen on the internet,

how whaling has changed,
they are of *least concern*.

Once mistaken for fin or blue,
their meat is most plentiful

hanging behind glass cases,
songless. Give a white man a knife,

a lance with exploding tip,
a star or shield-shaped badge—

Who won't he kill?

Narwhal

Monodon monoceros

Nar in Hindi means
    man as *whal* is *whale*
in some white
    tongue. What is manly
about me—
    my tusking other bulls
to communicate chemistry
    of saline in microchannels?
How long did it take
    your blond world
to see my bone
    as commodity, to saw it
from my head and
    present it to the king
of Denmark?
    My helical tusk
is canine and I've
    transformed too
in a frozen series
    of metamorphic snapshots
into a magic-
    blooded equestrian
into terror into
    ignorance

of what leviathan
    cravings lurk.
Sometimes we die
    from suffocation when
ice freezes over
    the sea's face.
Sometimes dancers'
    scarves strangle to death,
Like you I'm not
    man. It just takes time
for the next
    transformation
into whale fall
    where immortality
persists. You paint
    silks of half-
fish women,
    and pray to never
fall into abyss.

Noc

Delphinapterus leucas

According to the Smithsonian
from 1977-1980, six belugas
became US Cold-Op recruits,
and Noc learned to fall out
of canary-song and into mimicking
the naval officers who taught him
to spy underwater off
San Clemente Island and
to understand hand signals
and short commands during training
tests. In 1984 one trainer,
underwater close to Noc's
enclosure, heard the beluga
command him to *Get out!*
I am surprised by the arbitrary
ecology of language, how it holds
the universe, nirvana, and nothing
simultaneously and how
this beluga deciphered connection
between command and action.
And how Noc, NOC, No-C,
as in no-see, as in no-see-um,
reached out from its own
galaxy to express urgency. Again,

I make this human, looking
for metaphor and intention:
the wonder that the beluga
under imperial control,
in an ocean trampled as both
dump and battleground,
imitated human speech
through phonic lips enough
to say the phrase, *Get out!*
All to say that I agree
with the whale-addressed
Californian, not the US military
exploiting the sea and its beasts
for false freedoms—
how many people perished
as captives of imperialists—
but rather, I agree,
when a whale speaks
your language, what else
can you do but obey?

North Atlantic Right Whale

Eubalaena glacialis

"By the early 1890s, commercial whalers had hunted North Atlantic right whales to the brink of extinction. (They got their name from being the "right" whales to hunt because they floated when they were killed.)"
—NOAA Fisheries

The right whale to kill,
they float to be flensed

dorsal-less as they migrate along
the coast from the Caribbean

to Massachusetts, no longer
alive in the North Pacific,
hunted into silence.

The wage of shore-
hugging journey in harpooner-logic

is to slay from shore
and boat, to *try out* skins

in strips like bandages
for its bright honey,

to fuel lanterns. Right whales,
baleen whales but not

rorqual, number three hundred
in the Atlantic, struck

by vessels and tangled
in fishing gear still.

On the Flagler pier
a man pulls up shark after
shark on his line as the ocean

tongues the dock,
the entire boardwalk sways.

Those seasoned returnees
are already starving ghosts.

Northern Resident Orca

Orcinus orca

Some are lonely before
they know. An orca
separated from his pod
calls out every night
as scientists listen
underwater to his song
ricochet and break
against Vancouver rocks.
What song do I scatter
in my sleep; do I tuck
as coral polyps into the dark
quiet to root and reef
in these shallows? Who
do I want to hear this
while I bottom in the Pacific?
Is it still song if no one
understands my lyrics,
translates my extinct language,
if my tongue is an isolate
what is a curse; what is reunion
if there was never a pod,
but a fiction?

Omura's Whale

Balaenoptera omurai

In 2015 a new species of rorqual
spy hopped into human
consciousness. Once called
a dwarf fin whale we also mistook
it as a pygmy Bryde's Whale
but is more closely related
to the blue, and still one
of the *least known whale species*
according to marine biologists,
with asymmetric coloration,
up to forty feet long
according to some sources,
which causes me to ask
why it is so hard to see what
presents itself in complexity—
that we look for shapes
of other animals in the clouds;
why we need to define
hierarchies and family webs
in order for category and rule; why
we burn to remake others
in our own image and say
It's what God did when
we are both god and anti-god,

and in knowing itself surely,
we never will know. Despite
my *sapiens*-ness's bipedal
brain, I choose to remain hidden
from god and God. But like any
god I see you not as you
are, but as I am.

Pakicetus

The most basal ancestor
transitioned in Pakistan during the Eocene
from land mammal
to cetacean. Wolf-sized
its remains puzzle biologists
that anything could originate in South Asia
like a dense boned quadruped
that spread throughout the seas
like the assumption that Sanskrit
is a language from the Caucasus.
Taking to the water, diving
for fish after fish, its eyes turned
upward to see into the sky
from beneath. Disbelief
in Pakistan's value presents reason
for American drones and brown
terror in American streets. My mother calls,
some rebel flag followed
my sister home again, spitting sonar.
Like the ancestor, I hold
my breath and dive deep
and look up to see helicopters,
military satellites on the mauna,
and underwater, naval blasts.

Even in the middle of the Pacific,
code orange. Maybe I will
from filling my lungs, blood
rushing to my core,
into a finned thing,
transform.

Peter (Odontocetiphelia)

the bottlenose
isolated from the sea, has no choice:

Dolphinidae breathing
is voluntary. He falls

in love with a human,
Howe Lovatt, his only living contact

during a ten-week experiment
in 1965.

After access to females
proved too great
an interruption to lessons

on human speech,
the teacher pleasures her captive,
now called Pete,

manually.

After the bond shatters and Lovatt
publishes her findings,

she admits sex with *Tursiops truncatus*
to be precious, even gentle.

Pete sinks
to the bottom of his tank
and refuses air.

Pygmy Right Whale

Caperea marginata

"It's the last survivor of quite an ancient lineage that until now no one thought was around."
—Felix Marx, of the University of Otago, Aotearoa

So much is not clear
of ancient lineage. Is the ocean
too rich with nutrients or
is the whale's molecular
makeup and bone structure
not echoed in any other
species? A question puzzles
scientists for many years.
This smallest of baleen
whales they assumed to belong
to the Right Whale's taxonomic
category despite a falcate
dorsal fin, its mouth's curve
serving as a shibboleth.
What we can't make out
at first sight our brains
assimilate like how once
Justin imitated what he thought
an "Indian" sounded like

to mock my mother, whose
actual speech, like hurricane
or storm-bird, is from continents
away. *I don't like Muslims*
he said in Orlando. What did he know
of kinds: Coolie or Desi, or
what foreignness obscured
my desire for the neighbor boy?
He could have called me any
convenient animal.
All of the Pygmy Right Whale's
genus have died out
leaving no trace of family
Cetotheriidae—
its name scientists call
a *wastebasket genus* like
the term *South Asian* or
Middle Eastern or *faggot*
a category used to classify
what brown they see
and do not understand.

Pygmy Sperm Whale

Kogia breviceps

The most commonly stranded
cetacean in the Southeast,
this dwarf, though not
the dwarf sperm whale who
is an altogether separate species,
named for the spermaceti
that assists in echolocation,
is also known for its intestinal
sac that stores up to three
gallons of what NOAA calls
reddish-brown liquid and employs
a *squid tactic* of clouding the water
in a murky veil should some threat
encroach, though its main
environmental threats are, you
guessed it, human:
entanglements in tackle,
gear, and vessel strikes—
what a marvel of sperm and shit,
the whale is a fetish
of its range from the Caribbean,
to the Gulf of Mexico,
to the Atlantic, to the Pacific,
its entire eleven and a half

feet and one thousand pounds
make it relatively *cute*,
and charismatic with
a rounded dorsal, wilting ashore,
until the tractors come
to pull it away like in Indialantic,
Florida, or to euthanize
a stranded individual bashed
against the rocks in Malibu, where,
about this species, yes, but
also about how to protect
any blessed thing that blows
its own shofar in praise
of the Lord of Life
and Death, that pulses out
its timbrel, of those in dance
halleluhu hallelujah as a crown,
we know nothing and
care even less.

Rodhocetus balochistanensis

We all start out as wolves
stalking what prayers we can—
whether for benefit of others
or for my own melody's sake
after the kill, I eat my tongue
wet with blood and staccato
clicks. I survive by ignoring
the fires, all nature telling me
a mass extinction looms
and I should drop my flowers
and run. It's no small chance,
older than *Ambulocetus*,
this fanged whale's name refers to its
arched back, perhaps in supplication
perhaps part prolepsis
for the humpback and in this very song
and at the end of this line
I am fishing for transmogrification
in which you, reader,
hold your breath, startled
at being so addressed,
hook a flaming building
and are surprised
that in a window you see

a mirror and a face
that is your own,
prostrating before the altar
of your own desire—
let's be honest—
once for the benefit
of all but now
actually just
for yourself.

Sei Whale

Balaenoptera borealis

A die-off in 2015
leaves scientists stunned.
Three hundred thirty-seven
bodies turn white
on Patagonian fjord banks.
The largest stranding in history
by the third largest
rorqual, sixty-four foot,
the fastest cetacean, though
a sprinter; its throat furrows
allow mouthing hundreds
of gallons at a time, to expel
saline and to swallow krill
and schooling fish. Unable
to get close to the death
field, biologists posit
toxic blooms of red
tide slew great numbers
three to five million years ago,
fossils stud the Atacama,
whale bluish-grey now stone
color; yet they say nothing
about how in the mid 1900s
the exploding harpoon tip

made blossoms of skin
bloom and blood
in peals and petals
of blubber. Welcome
to the rose garden. Welcome
to the palimpsest. Someone else
now tends the petroleum beds,
a new garden planted on top of the old.
Come dry on land into a sea
change the way minerals
replace calcium on fallen
bones or the how
fact becomes story until
species die out: slow
at first *it's not your fault, you recycle,*
you use paper straws.

Short-Finned Pilot Whale

Globicephala macrorhynchus

Why they follow their kin onto land,
scientists cannot fathom.

You take to eating sticks
to kindle fire inside your torso,

lava through your veins. You
crave eruption. In the evening

you sit on the bluff;
name the stars you can see—

naked and asteroidal until
morning reaches out and plucks Lyra,

to save you from lack of touch,
you are Arion scattering

poems in the wind. You lost
your map, eardrums burst

from falling down the stairs
after the last man. His rum-bottle-green

whales breach the surface
of your skin still, scarred

onto your meridians. You watch a pod
of blackfish leap one by one,

each one following the other's distress,
onto the sand in the sun-fire,

bodies drying on the beach—
each one hungry for the other.

Sperm Whale

Physeter macrocephalus

A sperm whale's coda
kicks your chest
like a horse's hoof,
its beam of sound
lights the deep sea.
His words, words
that bear end: *let there be*
no longer and you two
were no longer. Biologists say
the whale call is *the loudest sound*
in the world though only know
that it travels the deep
until everything is clear,
but not its purpose—
a map of topography, of secrets
that no longer remain
hidden like that longing
you sound into:
a cloud garlands the mountain,
his coffee cup, now cold
as rain, and sudden night—
bioluminescence—jasmine bloom—

Timingala

But if I to go into Sanskrit—
which some believe was a language
never spoken until ritual, yet others
use the language of the devas to pronounce
others inferior, as if one could come
from the feet of Manu, from his thighs,
his arms, or his head, as though
there are others born outside of this
human construction, lesser than even
the servant—I will have to continue
my speaking in shortcuts, my impulse
to language, impulsive and machinist: for
every utterance precludes the pre-
utterance that there a silence existed
before the great whale or large fish,
before it, the breath that was drawn
and made through its drawing as if
this were the Divine database or
the Divine Spark or that big bang or
the *Kun Faya Kun* is the seat
of divinity instead of being
mere lung; but if I look back, there
is no end to the water cycle of that book
of breathing or precursor to even

that book, this whole endeavor sits
    at the seafloor, becomes monstrous
and fabulous, the way I use Google
    to look words like *chilichima* up, one
of the most ancient of tongues regenerated
    by the plumbing of the water column
of human memory's reservoir.

Varuna

Aditya's chariot enters
and you close your aqua curtains
about him. I water
my potted sanjivini herb
and drown it. I'm no King Rama,
not one to revive my own brother
poisoned on the battlefield,
I'd watch him succumb, watch
his throat blue. O Guru,
ishta-deva, cyclical god of rain
and hurricane, tidal god
of exile and despair,
bhakti's silt-bhajans bury your Veda,
your name vestigial
as my own tail. God,
who controls the makar
who causes stones to float, who spurs
walls of water to decimate
archipelagoes in one hot heave,
you inter bodies frozen
in motion. In your chest
you pressure proto-flukes
into crude oil. At which temple
should I bow my head,

god of life, ravishing god
of destruction, from you
all life flows, who brings joy
in excess brings death?
Even if I am Kabir's saint
who sees the ocean in the drop,
still I lose hind limbs
I grew for epochs. My prayer
to you is prayer to myself.

Water-Owl, Cuvier's Beaked Whale

Ziphius cavirostris

If only I could explain
without a sonic blast
that makes crumble
internal tympani; once
the owl-headed, fish-bodied,
beaked whale was known
for diving up to two-hundred-
twenty-two minutes, its diet
and circulation adapted
for this life; the visited world
is not its home—
What can we know about
these goose-rostrumed,
sword bearing Ziphiidae,
distributed worldwide,
diving so deep and for so long
that we cannot observe them
with regularity. When skulls
first appeared, legible, Cuvier
believed them already extinct
and now, they are of least concern,
strange how what we do not hear
does not concern us; why

does my eager heart always
lament language loss—
that the English-speaking
America is not my home
or that adaptation
is without complication?
When I think of the deepest
dive in the mammalian
world, I hear Antonio Gramsci
who developed the term
hegemonic pressure, how
underwater it works to consolidate
mass and to influence the body
into surviving the inhospitable
increase of gravity
in all dimensions
but in my home, it looks like
my mother's disparaging remark about
Bollywood songs, *too slow,*
too whiny, while I play
Kun Faya Kun for my three-
year-old nephew—
Empire's small victories

enthroned in our throats and how
this adaptation of my mother's
comments betrays her own
secret white wish and distaste
for her own difference
she still passes down as
a genetic mutation even though
she cannot be anything other
than herself, the mother
of two sons: one who ran away
to India and the other
who scratched blood
from a police officer's wrist
after headbutting his own son;
mother to a daughter who stayed
to serve the family's splintering hull—
and this is pressure: subtle
and scarring our skins white
as though cookie cutter sharks
tear from us our brown dermis
while we are still living—
a pressure that is invisible
at first but reverberates

louder with each generation
descending into a family
whose youngest teach their friends
to mispronounce their names.

Wholphin: Kekaimalu

Yours is the god
of storm, the moon's
lover, the untamed
god, but they name
you to placate, to pacify,
praying you would
remain amnesiac to your own
swells now specter,
a name itself a cage,
a cement tank to contain
your wild in Sea Life
Park who says you
would be endangered
in the wild, that you would
not exist at all if not
for the colonizing hand
that guided Tanui Hahai's,
your father's, false killer
whale penis into Punahele,
your bottlenose mother,
her womb an occupied
wound, an overthrown
sovereignty echoic

of the gouged earth turned
pool, painted turquoise
you now lap in circles,
your rostrum whitening
with scars, your name
The Peaceful Sea but the sea
is rage and might and
on the seaside it chews cars
into red dust, it swallows
aircraft carriers, breaks
nations and licks roads
into beach, so your wild
can't be held in one
name when inside of you
a typhoon brews and when
you jump through trainer's rings
and launch basketballs
into the sky you glimpse
over the Waimānalo cliff, ocean
pounding the proudest stone
into sand and off
in the distance you see
and remember: a humpback

breaches, a circle of white,
a cage of mist, soon broken
into salt and ghosts.

Yangtze River Dolphin

Lipotes vexillifer

—extinct—

Notes

I composed and edited these poems from 2013-2025 in Honolulu, Waimea, Niu Valley, Mānoa, Ōtepoti (Dunedin), Tāmaki Makaurau (Aukland) Aotearoa, Ft. Walton Beach, Casselberry, Orlando, Miami, Queens, New York City, Opelika, Auburn, Georgetown, Guyana, Malden, Boston, Newburyport, Provincetown, Gambier, Seattle, Portland, Santa Barbara, Juneau, Denver, and Boulder.

I used my own first-hand observations of what cetacean and cultural lives I encountered in my travels and from research into the natural history and news articles about the various species mentioned here. Along with these specific sites and articles listed, I also used information found in the books:

The Lives of Hawaiʻi's Dolphins and Whales: Natural History and Conservation by Robin W. Baird
Fathoms: The World in the Whale by Rebecca Giggs
The Whale: In Search of the Giants of the Sea by Philip Hoare
The Killer Whale Who Changed the World by Mark Leiren-Young
The Natural History of the Whale by L. Harrison Matthews
How to Speak Whale: A Voyage into the Future of Animal Communication by Tom Mustill
Spying on Whales: The Past, Present, and Future of Earth's Most Awesome Creatures by Nick Pyenson
The Cultural Lives of Whales and Dolphins by Hal Whitehead and Luke Rendell
Whale Music: Thousand Mile Songs in a Sea of Sound by David Rothenberg

Whale Song (Object Lessons) by Margret Grebowicz

*

"*Ambulocetus natans*" uses information found in Wikipedia and in: Madar, S. I., et al. "Additional Holotype Remains of Ambulocetus Natans (Cetacea, Ambulocetidae), and Their Implications for Locomotion in Early Whales." *Journal of Vertebrate Paleontology*, vol. 22, no. 2, 2002, pp. 405–22.

"*Basilosaurus cetoides*" uses information found in the article "Museum's Collection Spotlight" on the University of Alabama's website.

"Bowhead Whale" relies on the finding of fragments from a 250-year-old harpoon point in the shoulder bone of a bowhead whale in Alaska. Information taken from the website Awesome Ocean.

"Boto" is another name for the pink-skinned Amazon River dolphin, who legend says is a shapeshifter that appears on land to seduce and impregnate people before abandoning them and returning to the river.

"Bryde's Whale" uses information found in NOAA Fisheries site.

"Common Bottlenose Dolphin" uses information found in "SEDUCE ME: Dolphin" from Green Porno's Isabella Rossellni, available on Youtube and the article "Bottlenose Dolphins Can Identify Friends by Tasting Their Urine" from *NewScientist*.

"Costero" uses information form Wikipedia and *The Online Guide to the Animals of Trinidad and Tobago* published by The University of the West Indies.

"Devilfish" uses information from the article "Whale Takes Boatload of Tourists for the Ride of Their Lives" from *The New York Post*.

"*Dorudon serratus*" uses information found in Wikipedia.

"False Killer Whale" uses information found in *Voices in the Ocean: A Journey into the Wild and Haunting World of Dolphins* by Susan Casey and from the website for the non-profit Whale and Dolphin Conservation.

"Franciscana" uses information found in the 2016 *The Washington Post* article "Endangered Baby Dolphin Dies after Swimmers Pass It around for Selfies."

"Gulf Whale (Rice's Whale)" uses information from the essay by Julia-Claire Evans, "Meet the New Species of Endangered Whale Discovered in the Gulf of Mexico" posted on the National Wildlife Federation's blog.

"Hybrid Unidentified Whale" uses information that can be found in *The Guardian* article "The Search for the Loneliest Whale in the World."

"Iberian Orca" uses information found in the *Smithsonian Magazine* called "Orca Rams into Yacht Near Scotland, Suggesting the Behavior May Be Spreading."

"*Indohyus indirae*" uses information found in the online encyclopedia, Alchetron.

"Irawaddy Dolphin" uses information found on the World Wildlife Fund's website.

"Makara" is named after the vahana of the goddess Ganga (the goddess of the Ganges River) and is written in form of a vandana.

"Manatee" uses information found in Wikipedia and in the CBS News Boston article called "Manatee Sightings Reported off Cape Cod."

"Minke Whale" uses information found in *Hakai Magazine's* article called "Learn to Grunt and Growl like an Antarctic Minke Whale."

"Noc" uses information found in the 2014 *Smithsonian Magazine* article called "The Story of One Whale Who Tried to Bridge the Linguistic Divide Between Animals and Humans."

"Northern Resident Orca" uses information found in the 2006 and 2023 *Vancouver Sun* article "Luna Could 'Speak' Sea Lion: Lonely Whale Mimicked Their Barking, Scientists Claim."

"Omura's Whale" uses information from Wikipedia and from WDC (Whale and Dolphin Conservation)'s website.

"Peter (Odonticetiphelia)" uses information found in Susan Casey's *Voices in the Ocean: A Journey into the Wild and Haunting World of Dolphins* and in the article "How a Science Experiment Led to Sexual Encounters Between a Woman and a Dolphin" from *The Atlantic*.

"Pygmy Right Whale" uses information from the University of Otago's article "Whale of a Debate Put to Rest" and from the *NBC* article "Found: Whale Thought Extinct for 2 Million Years."

"Pygmy Sperm Whale" uses information found in NOAA Fisheries site.

"Sei Whale" uses information found in *The Guardian* article from 2015 called "337 Whales Dead in Chile in One of History's Biggest Beachings."

"Sperm Whale" uses information found in the Guinness World Records.

"Varuna" is the named after the Vedic Sea god.

"Water-owl, Cuvier's Beaked Whale" uses information found in NOAA Fisheries site.

Acknowledgments

Thanks to the editors of these journals where poems previously appeared—oftentimes in different versions: *About Place Journal, Academy of American Poets Poem-a-Day, Action, Spectacle, Bamboo Ridge Journal, Black Warrior Review, The Cincinnati Review, Congeries: An Online Artifact of Connotations Press, Copper Nickel, The Dodge, The DMQ Review, Eleven Eleven, Killer Whale Journal, Massachusetts Review, Michigan Quarterly Review, Moko: Caribbean Arts and Letters, Poemeleon, Raleigh Review, Saw Palm: Florida Literature and Art, Sixth Finch, Southern Humanities Review, SPECS Journal, Summit Magazine, Underblong,* and *wildness.*

Thanks to the editors of the anthologies *GO HOME!,* and *After Moby Dick: An Anthology of New Poetry.*

Thanks to the Massachusetts Cultural Council's Artists Fellowship for their generous funding.

Abiding love and appreciation for the Four Way Books family including Martha Rhodes, Ryan Murphy, Hannah Matheson, Bridget Bell, and Trish Marshall.

Loving gratitude to Divya Victor, Charif Shanahan, and No'u Revilla for their love and care.

Special thanks to my early readers: Elizabeth Bradfield, Mary Kovaleski Byrnes, Joanna Gordon, Carlie Hoffman, Akta Kaushal, Amalia Bueno,

Shikha Malaviya, No'u Revilla, Anjoli Roy, Samuel Skold, Adeeba Shahid Talukder, Rushi Vyas, Kate Beutner, Katie Williams, Julie Carr, Ruth Ellen Kocher, Roy Kamada, Marcelo Hernandez Castillo, Angela Winsor, Andre Bagoo, Shivanee Ramlochan, and Andil Gosine.

About the Author

Poet, memoirist, and translator, Rajiv Mohabir is the author of five books of poetry and has been awarded two gold medals from the Foreword INDIES and Eric Hoffer Medal Provocateur. His other honors include being a finalist for the National Book Critics Circle Award, the PEN/America Open Book Award, the Lambda Literary Award, the Randy Shilts Award for Gay Nonfiction, and both second place and finalist for the Guyana Prize for Literature. His translations have won the Harold Morton Landon Translation Award from the Academy of American Poets. Currently he teaches poetry at the University of Colorado Boulder.

We are also grateful to those individuals who participated in our Build a Book Program. They are:

Anonymous (5), Robert Abrams, Debra Allbery, Maggie Anderson, Jean Ball, Sally Ball, Adria Bernardi, Richard Blanchard, Laurel Blossom, Lee Briccetti, Anne Babson Carter, Jennifer Christman, Aaron Coleman, Peter Coyote, Elinor Cramer, Michael Anna de Armas, Brian Komei Dempster, Patrick Donnelly, Lynn Emanuel, Joan Frank, Rigoberto Gonzalez, Elizabeth T. Gray Jr., David and Joan Grubin, Naomi Guttman and Jonathan Mead, Beth Harrison, Jeffrey Harrison, KT Herr, Carlie Hoffman, Elizabeth Jackson, Linda Susan Jackson, Marilyn Johnson, Deborah Jonas-Walsh, Maeve Kinkead, David Lee and Jamila Trindle, Rodney Terich Leonard, Jen Levitt, Howard Levy, Owen Lewis and Susan Ennis, Ralph and Mary Ann Lowen, Maja Lukic, Ricardo Alberto Maldonado, Cleopatra Mathis, Victoria McCoy, Lupe Mendez, Mary Jane Nealon, Nicole Nevadunsky, Kimberly Nunes, Cathy McArthur Palermo, Veronica Patterson, Eileen Pollack, Martha Rhodes, Soraya Shalforoosh, Sarah Stone, Yerra Sugarman, Marjorie and Lew Tesser, Reed Turchi, Maria Walsh, and Calvin Wei